Franklin E. Denton

Prospectus of the National Convention,

League of Republican clubs, Cleveland, June 19, 20, 21, 1895. Compiled for

use of delegates, and containing a history of the convention city

Franklin E. Denton

Prospectus of the National Convention,
League of Republican clubs, Cleveland, June 19, 20, 21, 1895. Compiled for use of delegates, and containing a history of the convention city

ISBN/EAN: 9783337424374

Printed in Europe, USA, Canada, Australia, Japan

Cover: Foto ©Suzi / pixelio.de

More available books at **www.hansebooks.com**

PROSPECTUS

OF THE

NATIONAL CONVENTION

League of Republican Clubs,

CLEVELAND, JUNE 19, 20, 21, 1895.

COMPILED FOR USE OF DELEGATES, AND CONTAINING
A HISTORY OF THE CONVENTION CITY, ILLUS-
TRATIONS OF PRINCIPAL POINTS OF
INTEREST, AND INFORMATION OF
USE TO SIGHT-SEERS.

National Executive and Local Entertainment Committees' Programs.

CLEVELAND, O.

THE CLEVELAND PRINTING & PUBLISHING CO.

1895.

W. W. TRACY,

CHICAGO,

President Republican National League.

Republican National League,

Wednesday, June 19, 1895.

CALL FOR THE CONVENTION.

To Republican State Leagues, League Clubs and all Republicans :

In compliance with a provision of the constitution of the Republican National League establishing an annual convention, and in accordance with the instructions of the last National Convention at Denver, the Eighth Annual Convention of the Republican National League of the United States is hereby called to meet in the city of *Cleveland, Wednesday, June 19, 1895, at 10 A. M.*, and continue its sessions until its business is completed.

The ratio of representation will be six delegates-at-large from each State and Territory, four from each congressional district, and one delegate from each College Club, represented by one of its own members in the Annual Convention of the American Republican College League for 1895. The following are *ex officio* delegates, viz: the President, Secretary and Treasurer of the National League ; one Vice-President and one Executive member of the National organization from each State and Territory, and the President and Secretary of each State and Territorial League, making four *ex officio* delegates from each. This gives each State practically ten delegates-at-large in addition to the four from each congressional district. The total representation will exceed two thousand delegates, with an equal number of alternates.

The business of the meeting will include reports from the officers of the League, the election of officers, vice-presidents and members of the executive committee for the ensuing year ; the designation or reference of the time and place for the next National League Convention ; a general discussion of League work, party policies and organization ; the formation of a plan of campaign, with special reference to the presidential year, and a consideration of such other questions as the convention may deem proper.

Special railroad rates have been secured for the convention,

D. D. WOODMANSEE,

CINCINNATI,

President Ohio Republican League.

E. J. MILLER,

COLUMBUS,

Secretary Ohio Republican League.

and information concerning the same will be supplied by the various State League officials, or direct from these headquarters.

By order of the Executive Committee.

W. W. TRACY, *President.*

A. B. HUMPHREY, *Secretary.*

National Headquarters, 140 Dearborn Street, Chicago.

SPECIAL ANNOUNCEMENTS.

1. It is proposed to take three days for the convention, to give ample time for the consideration of questions of special interest to the party at this time.

2. There will be excursions about Cleveland to Put-in-Bay in Lake Erie, Niagara Falls and Chautauqua if desired.

3. RAILROADS—The Central Traffic Association has granted a one-fare rate for the round trip in the territory east of Chicago, St. Louis and Cairo, and north of the Ohio river to Buffalo and Pittsburg, including Michigan. The Trunk Line Association has granted a rate of full fare going, and one-third fare returning, in the territory between New York, Buffalo and Pittsburg. It is expected that the Passenger Associations representing New England and the South and West will grant equally favorable or better terms.

4. A special train will probably be run from Denver to accommodate the western delegates. Parties wishing to join this train should correspond with C. W. Varnum, State League Secretary, Denver, Colo. Special trains will probably be run from New York, Philadelphia, Chicago, Nashville, Louisville, Pittsburg, and Cincinnati.

5. Some of the Minnesota and northwestern delegates are arranging to come by boat around the Great Lakes.

6. National and State League officials, whose names will be found on another page, will arrange for transportation of delegates by States.

7. The hotels at Cleveland are excellent and numerous, and prices will range from $1.50 to $4.00 per day. As this will be the largest League convention ever held, delegates are advised to engage accommodations in advance.

8. One or more mass meetings will be held and will be addressed by some of the best speakers in the United States.

9. The citizens of Cleveland are preparing a grand entertainment for the delegates.

6

FACTS.

Fact 1 Selected by the U. S. Government to run the fast mail trains.

Fact 2 Is the only double-track line between Cleveland and the East or West.

Fact 3 Is the route of the famous 24 hour train between Chicago and New York.

Fact 4 Conceded by travelers everywhere to be the most comfortable route in America.

Fact 5 It runs Through Sleeping Cars between Cleveland, Chicago, Buffalo and New York, and Boston.

The
Lake Shore &
Michigan Southern
Railway.

10. The National League headquarters during convention week will be at the Hollenden Hotel, Cleveland.

11. For all local information about hotels, excursions, etc., address F. H. Morris, Chairman, Arcade Bldg., Cleveland, Ohio.

NATIONAL CONVENTIONS OF THE LEAGUE.

The Republican League of the United States was organized in Chickering Hall, New York City, December 15th-17th, 1887, by delegates from about 350 Republican Clubs of the United States, assembled in national convention pursuant to a call issued by the Republican Club of New York City. National conventions have since been held in Baltimore, Md., February 28, 1889; Nashville, Tenn., March 4, 1890; Cincinnati, O., April 23, 1891; Buffalo, N. Y., September 16, 1892; Louisville, Ky., May 10, 1893; Denver, Colo., June 26, 1894. The Eighth Annual Convention will be held in Cleveland, O., June 19, 1895.

THE REPUBLICAN LEAGUE PLAN.

The League is founded on the rights and duties of the individual citizens, the solid corner-stone of Republicanism, and aims to enlist all Republican forces as auxiliaries of the regular party organization. Its chief business is to elect candidates and not to nominate them.

1. The *Local Club* is composed of *individuals*, with equal voice in all its affairs.

2. The *State League* is composed of the *Local Clubs* of each State, and each club has personal representation at all State conventions and elections of officers and committees.

3. The *National League* is composed of one *State League* from each State and Territory in the United States, and derives its authority from instructions given and committees elected by representatives from each State and Territorial League in National Convention assembled.

The League and all its branches, Local, State and National, has only one grand aim, namely: To advocate, promote and maintain the principles of Republicanism as enunciated by the Republican party.

For plan of organization and form of constitution, address, A. B. Humphrey, National Secretary, 140 Dearborn Street, Chicago, Illinois.

CHASE STEWART,

SPRINGFIELD,

Treasurer Ohio Republican League

CHARLES F. LEACH,

CLEVELAND,

First Vice-President Ohio Republican League.

FRANK P. RICHTER,

HAMILTON,

Second Vice-President Ohio Republican League.

A

National
Business

BASED ON

A

National
Reputation

IS ONE OF THE REASONS WHY

The Official Programme

OF THE

REPUBLICAN NATIONAL LEAGUE

APPROPRIATELY BEARS THE IMPRINT OF

. . The . .

Cleveland Printing & Publishing Co.

OFFICE AND WORKS,

27, 29 and 31 Vincent Street,

CLEVELAND, O.

W. M. DAY, President.
F. J. STARAL, V. P. and Gen'l Manager.
G. H. GARDNER, Sec'y and Treas.
A. WINTENBERG, Sup't.

New York Office,
33 Union Square.

Chicago Office,
1142 Monadnock Block.

11

OHIO REPUBLICAN LEAGUE.

The organization of the Ohio Republican League was the outgrowth of a conviction that club work was the most effective agency to party success. No substantial victory had been won by the Republican party in this State but that had upon it the impress of the aid that was given to it by the various Republican clubs. In order that this influence might be centralized, and that its real power might be enlarged, all of these clubs were put into one organization, since which time they have been known as the League of Clubs.

The Ohio Republican League was born January 11, 1886. Its work was extended into every county and city in the State, and by and by a political organization of much magnitude had proved itself to be of far greater importance than was ever anticipated by its warmest friends. It has had its seasons of depression as well as of lively activity, but it has always been ready and willing to do its full share of party service. It was this same spirit of club organization that spread from State to State, and, as a result, the National Republican League was organized upon a larger scale, but upon the same basis, and for the same purposes. It is unnecessary, at this time, to refer to the success of that larger enterprise, for its history has been a great political triumph, which is well known to all Republicans.

It is possible that the plans of the Ohio Republican League might not be void of interest to club workers in other States. Under its constitution, any active Republican Club in the State, of at least thirty members, is entitled to membership upon paying an annual assessment of $5.00. The League holds a State Convention annually, on Lincoln's birthday, February 12th.

Childs, Groff & Co.

MANUFACTURERS

AND

JOBBERS OF

Boots and Shoes.

WESTERN RUBBER AGENCY

FOR THE SALE OF

Rubber Boots and Shoes

MADE BY

THE BOSTON RUBBER SHOE CO.

82 and 84 Bank St.,

CLEVELAND,   -   OHIO.

13

Each club, regardless of its number of members, is entitled to ten delegates in that convention. It has been the custom of the League to hold the annual Lincoln Day Banquet on the evening of the State Convention, and this banquet has become recognized as one of the most interesting and important events in the political history of our State. The eloquence of our leaders, from various States of the Union, has often been heard at these banquets, and it is an occasion to which Ohioans look with great interest.

The President of the League annually appoints five representative Republicans as an Organization Committee, who are at the head of the work of bringing in new clubs. Recently, the Executive Committee has been enlarged to one member from each county in the State, and two members from those counties which have two Congressional districts. This Executive Committee is the great working force of the League, and the success of the League in any county depends largely upon the Executive Committeeman from that county, as well as upon the officers of the League. The convention held this year was one of much enthusiasm, and new clubs are constantly coming into the League.

The League does not pretend to be a distinct political organization, but simply tenders its services to the regular party organization, and the harmony which exists between the League and the regular campaign organization has been productive of much good. They work together, with the belief that the only object in view is to achieve party success by all honorable means.

The present officers of the League are alive to the duties that are upon them. The president, D. D. Woodmansee, of Cincinnati, has twice been elected to this important trust by the unanimous vote of our State Convention. In all of his efforts to develop the League, he has had the hearty co-operation of the Secretary, E. J. Miller, of Columbus, who has rendered faithful service to the League and the Republican party.

We believe that there is still a place for the League, and that new victories of our party will be won by its assistance. We believe that the magnificent Republican majority of '94, in this State, of more than 130,000, if not maintained, will decrease less speedily because the League is with us. Its future is what we make it. May it grow and prosper, and be to our party a constant source of strength and courage.

SAM. B. HILL,

CINCINNATI,

Third Vice-President Ohio Republican League.

W. B. GAITREE,

COLUMBUS,

Fourth Vice-President Ohio Republican League.

CUYAHOGA COUNTY SOLDIERS' AND SAILORS' MONUMENT,
CLEVELAND, O.

(View from Northeast.)

17

HISTORY OF THE LEAGUE MOVEMENT.

There is an appropriateness in the Republican League of the United States meeting in convention in Ohio, for the League movement is another of the many "Ohio ideas" which have made the Buckeye State famous.

By general consent, the credit of originating the present league movement is given to Mr. James Boyle, now private secretary of Governor McKinley. In the Fall of 1885, during the noted gubernatorial campaign of Hon. J. B. Foraker, Mr. Boyle, who was on the editorial staff of the Cincinnati *Commercial Gazette*, sent a communication to the chairman of the Election Committee of the Cincinnati Young Men's Blaine Club, suggesting the organization of a State League of all the permanent Republican Clubs in Ohio. The directors favored the idea, and a special committee was appointed to carry it into effect. Mr. Boyle was made chairman of the committee. The first thing he did was to secure endorsements from the leaders of the party in Ohio. Care was taken to explain that the intention was to allow every club to manage its own affairs, and that provision would be made to prevent the League interfering with the official machinery of the party, and also to prevent it being used to control nominations.

Subsequently, at a meeting of the representatives of the Young Men's Blaine Club, the Lincoln Club, the Sherman Club, of Cincinnati, and of the clubs of the Twelfth, Fourteenth and Sixteenth Wards of that city, Mr. Boyle was authorized, in the name of those organizations, to call a conference to "assemble in the office of the Secretary of State, Columbus, at five P. M., January 11, 1886 [when J. B. Foraker was inaugurated Governor], to consider the question of the formation of a league of all permanent Republican Clubs in the State. All such clubs in Ohio

are invited to send delegates (from one to five each) duly accredited." The conference was very largely attended, and it was unanimously and enthusiastically resolved to form a State League, and a committee was appointed to draft a constitution. Mr. Boyle was made chairman of the committee, and after a great deal of trouble and consideration, a constitution was framed.

Acting by authority of the conference of clubs referred to above, a call was issued on June 28, 1886, by James Boyle, Chairman, and Richard J. Fanning, Secretary of the Committee on Organization, for the first convention of the Ohio Republican League, to be held at Columbus, August 25, 1886, at the Garfield Club rooms, Columbus. The constitution, as drafted by the committee, was ratified. Article 2 read: "This League is organized for the advancement of the principles of the Republican party, and particularly for the formation, encouragement and enrollment of permanent Republican Clubs, and shall act in co-operation with the regular Republican committees." Article 3 read: " Any permanently organized Republican Club in the State of Ohio, having adopted a constitution and by-laws, is eligible for membership in this League." Hon. Daniel J. Ryan, then the Representative in the Legislature from Scioto County, was elected the first President of the League.

Thus was organized, on the 25th of August, 1886, the first State League of Republican Clubs. It will be observed that this organization contemplated a league of co-ordinate local and independent organizations, banded together for mutual benefit and for the benefit of the party at large, this system being in contradistinction from the other plans attempted as stated above, namely, bureaucratic, with a central body, having subordinate clubs or branches throughout the State or country. It was felt by those who organized the League that to be successful it must allow the widest possible latitude for local conditions and individual club autonomy, the prime condition of membership in the League being that each club having affiliation therewith should be *bona fide* Republican, and organized with a permanent intent. The constitution of the Ohio State League, as originally formed, has not been materially changed since then, and has been made the model of nearly all of the State Leagues throughout the country. The "Ohio idea" rapidly spread in the East and West.

LAKE IN WADE PARK. CASE SCHOOL IN DISTANCE.

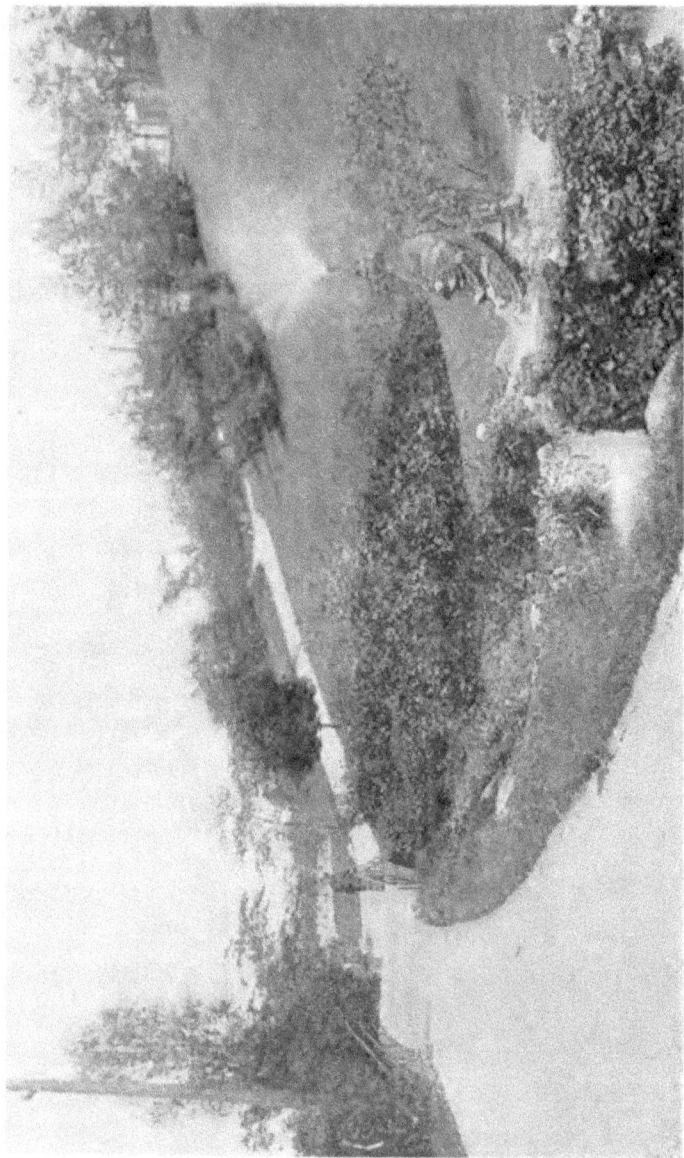

DRAGON FOUNTAIN, LAKE VIEW PARK.

23

The development of the State League into the National League is to be placed to the credit of the "Republican Club" of the City of New York. At a call of that organization, a national convention of State Leagues, and of individual clubs throughout the country, was held at Chickering Hall, New York City, on December 15, 16 and 17, 1887, and the Republican League of the United States was then and there formed. Hon. Daniel J. Ryan, President of the Ohio State League, was made Vice President of the convention, and Mr. Boyle was made Chairman of the Committee on National Organization, which reported the original constitution of the Republican League of the United States, and the Ohio plan of State organization was recommended as the model for other State Leagues.

VIEW IN RIVERSIDE CEMETERY.

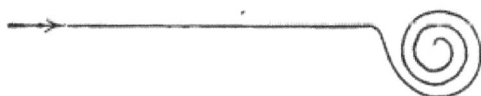

PROGRAM OF THE GENERAL COMMITTEE.

Wednesday, June 19.

10:00 A. M.—Session of the Convention, Music Hall.

1:00 P. M.—Short excursion to parks, factories, cemeteries, and suburbs.

2:00 P. M.—League picnic at Forest City Park; admission free to delegates. Concert by the Iowa State Band.

8:00 P. M.—Mass meeting at Music Hall.

8:00 P. M.—Open meeting and reception given by the Young Men's Foraker Club to the colored delegates, at Excelsior Hall, Erie street and Scovill avenue.

8:30 P. M.—Concert by Iowa State Band at Forest City Park.

Thursday, June 20.

9:00 A. M.—Short excursion to parks, factories, cemeteries, and suburbs.

11:00 A. M.—Excursion No. 1 upon Lake Erie, free to delegates, upon palace steamer City of Cleveland.

2:00 P. M.—Excursion No. 2, similar to No. 1.

2:00 P. M.—Open meeting at Music Hall, with speeches by prominent orators.

6:00 to 8:00 P. M.—Reception to the delegates at the Biclorama building, corner of Euclid avenue and Erie street.

8:30 P. M.—Banquet tendered the delegates at the Arcade, Euclid avenue and Superior street.

Friday, June 21.

10:00 A. M.—Session of the Convention, Music Hall.

2:00 P. M.—Session of the Convention, Music Hall.

Headquarters of General Entertainment Committee and Bureau of Information at 241 Arcade.

F. H. MORRIS, *Chairman*,   C. F. LEACH, *Treas.*,

H. N. HILL, *Sec'y.*

NICKEL PLATE

QUICK TIME — LOW RATES

THROUGH SLEEPING CARS
CHICAGO, BUFFALO,
NEW YORK & BOSTON
A SUPERB PASSENGER SERVICE

Solid Through Trains

BETWEEN

CHICAGO, NEW YORK AND BOSTON.

A Superb DINING CAR Service...

City Ticket Offices, 224 BANK ST., 534 PEARL ST. AND DEPOTS.

SEE THAT NAME

—Peerless?

—"*Just a Little Better Than the Best*"

. . . .

There's a Rakish Mount for You!

Please place your optics on that name,
Enduring as the vaulted sky,
Excelling *all* in worth and fame,
Receiving praise from far and nigh.
Let others talk as much they will,
E'en though their talk be smooth and sweet,
Since they have not "that name" to bill,
Scarce can they hope "that name" to beat.

PEERLESS MANUFACTURING CO.,

CLEVELAND, OHIO.

BY THE WAY, SEND FOR CATALOGUE.

27

GENERAL ENTERTAINMENT COMMITTEE OF 1895.

D. D. Woodmansee, Cincinnati; E. J. Miller, Columbus; F. P. Richter, Hamilton; S. B. Hill, Cincinnati; W. B. Gaitree, Columbus; Chase Stewart, Springfield; D. L. Sleeper, Athens; B. L. McElroy, Mt. Vernon; J. R. Knighton, Hamden; John L. Locke, Cambridge; S. J. Hathaway, Marietta; C. W. F. Dick, Akron; Harlan F. Burket, Findlay; James Boyle, Columbus; J. M. Ashley, Jr., Toledo; F. H. Morris, C. F. Leach, E. W. Doty, H. H. Burgess, W. A. Spilker, Martin Dodge, J. W. Hencke, Theo. McConnell, H. N. Hill, James Caldwell, J. A. Smith, Theo. Closse, W. J. Monks, C. W. Collister, J. J. Hogan, Hermann Zapf, A. McAllister, A. E. Akins, W. E. Cubben, T. W. Hill, H. A. Griffin, James W. Stewart, Emil Joseph, W. J. Akers, Luther Allen.

EXECUTIVE COMMITTEE.

F. H. Morris, E. W. Doty, James Caldwell, C. W. Collister, Theo. Closse, James W. Stewart.

FINANCE COMMITTEE.

A. McAllister, Chairman.

W. J. Akers, M. A. Hanna, O. C. Ringle, I. P. Lamson, C. B. Beach, T. E. Burton, Ferd W. Leek, M. T. Herrick, Wm. Greif, R. S. Hubbard, John C. Covert, F. DeH. Robison.

TICKET COMMITTEE.

M. A. Hanna, Chairman.

C. F. Leach, M. A. Bradley, H. D. Goulder, C. W. Chase, James Wood, S. H. Schmuck, A. E. Gilbert, J. A. Smith, Chas. F. Post, Geo. Gibson, H. R. Groff, M. J. Mandelbaum, C. C. Burnett, Luther Allen, H. E. Hill, S. H. Tolles, O. C. Ringle, Minor G. Norton, Mars Wagar, S. T. Denison, J. W. Moore, Jas. H. Hoyt, M. M. Hobart, M. A. Marks.

COMMITTEE ON SPEAKERS.

Hon. T. E. Burton.

COMMITTEE ON BANQUET.

W. J. Akers, Chairman.

B. D. Babcock, Chas. Wesley, Isaac Reynolds, Daniel Davis, M. A. Bradley, Wm. Edwards, L. M. Coe, J. J. Sullivan, Frank Brobst, Seth T. Paine, R. E. Gill, R. S. Aikenhead, John Tod, C. A. Brayton, H. C. Ellison.

28

29

COMMITTEE ON BADGES.

H. H. Stair, Chairman.

C. O. Bassett, Geo. Groll, O. M. McAninch.

COMMITTEE ON MUSIC.

Martin Dodge, Chairman.

J. F. Stair, W. R. Vorce, Sylvester Scovil, F. N. Wilcox, Ora J. Hoffman, Wm. J. Monks, Geo. Ford, Willard Abbott, Will R. Rose.

MENU COMMITTEE.

Elroy M. Avery, Chairman.

Ryerson Ritchie, Hermon A. Kelley, M. P. Mooney.

INTRAMURAL EXCURSION COMMITTEE.

Howard H. Burgess, Chairman.

John J. Stanley, Wm. Prescott, Geo. Mulhern, W. A. Spilker.

CONVENTION HALL COMMITTEE.

Wm. B. Wright, Chairman.

T. D. Brown, Thos. McCaslin, John Glover, David Nelson, C. A. Metcalf, Fred. Witt, Jos. Coghill, Chas. Gordon, S. A. Muhlhauser, Robert Simpson, W. K. Radcliffe.

COMMITTEE ON DECORATIONS.

L. N. Weber, Chairman.

Ed. O. Peets, F. C. Bate, Louis Malm, E. W. Horn, S. H. Cramer, F. E. Dellenbaugh, Geo. B. Tripp.

PAMPHLET AND PROSPECTUS COMMITTEE.

H. A. Griffin, Chairman.

W. M. Day, T. H. Rose, E. H. Baker, James Caldwell.

PRESS COMMITTEE.

E. W. Doty, Chairman.

A. E. Heiss, Ed. Botten, Edw. Wright, S. E. Kaiser, J. J. Spurgeon, S. T. Hughes, E. W. Bowers, Ed. B. Lilley, A. S. Van Duser, T. J. Rose, E. A. Roberts, Will R. Rose, Will S. Lloyd, Jacob Waldeck, Will Sage, A. E. Hyre, James Cockett, F. L. Willcutt, Jacob E. Mueller, Harry Nelson, C. M. Maedje, E. C. Forbes, H. C. Smith, J. C. Keffer, W. Scott Robison, Felix Rosenberg, Sam Oppenheimer, R. W. Wheelock, Hiram Straus, E. D. Peebles, Harry Leonard.

WELCOMING COMMITTEE.

T. D. Brown, Chairman, with one hundred assistants.

GARFIELD MONUMENT.

JAMES H. HOYT, ESQ.

Mr. Hoyt has achieved a place in the public life of this State by an entirely natural and unforced process that justly entitles him to rank with the best of Ohio's sons. It is true, that the full recognition of his worth and strength has come to many of his fellow-citizens like an awakening or a new idea; but this is because he has heretofore refused to be considered for positions of public trust and responsibility, which would have made his ability and energy more widely known, and not because of any doubt as to his qualifications for the highest public service among those who constitute the large circle of his social and professional acquaintances.

Mr. Hoyt's family is one of the oldest and most respected in this part of the State. His father, recently deceased, James M. Hoyt, was a prominent member of the bar, held important offices of trust, and was a man of marked literary ability. James H. Hoyt, Esq., is the third of four sons, and is forty-two years of age. Rev. Dr. Wayland Hoyt, of Minneapolis, and Colgate Hoyt, of New York, are the best known of his brothers. He graduated in the public schools of this city, attended the Harvard Law School, and after admission to the bar engaged actively in the practice of his profession. He is now senior member of the well-known law firm of Hoyt, Dustin & Kelley, and has achieved a high reputation in his profession, many large interests being entrusted to his care. Some able men have escaped distinction because of inability to give fluent and forcible expression to their knowledge or ideas. Such is not the case with Mr. Hoyt. His exceptional ability as an orator has, in fact, directed attention to him as a man with broad views, undoubted intellectual strength, and well-disciplined mental processes. He is one of the most interesting, entertaining and instructive speakers in Ohio, and the Buckeye State ranks second to none in the Union in that respect. There seems to be no limit to the resources of his well-stored mind, so that whatever the occasion that calls him to the platform, or however short the notice, he is always able to please and to instruct. The people of Cincinnati were treated to an exhibition of Mr. Hoyt's oratorical powers on the occasion of the banquet given to the visiting business men of Cleveland by the Cincinnati Chamber of Commerce a few weeks ago. It was a wonderful speech. Its purpose, as may well be supposed, was to create a kindly feeling between the business men of the two cities, and the manifestations of amity and enthusiasm it aroused will never be forgotten by those present. When Mr. Hoyt sat down, Cincinnati announced that her sweet sister Cleveland could have anything that the orator of the evening desired.

Mr. Hoyt has always been an active Republican. There is no taint of Mugwumpery upon his political garments. His talents and means have repeatedly been employed in the defense of Republican principles. He is an active member of the leading Republican organizations of the city, and is always found at the front when there is need of wise counsel and arduous service.

THE CUYAHOGA VALLEY, CLEVELAND, IN 1851.

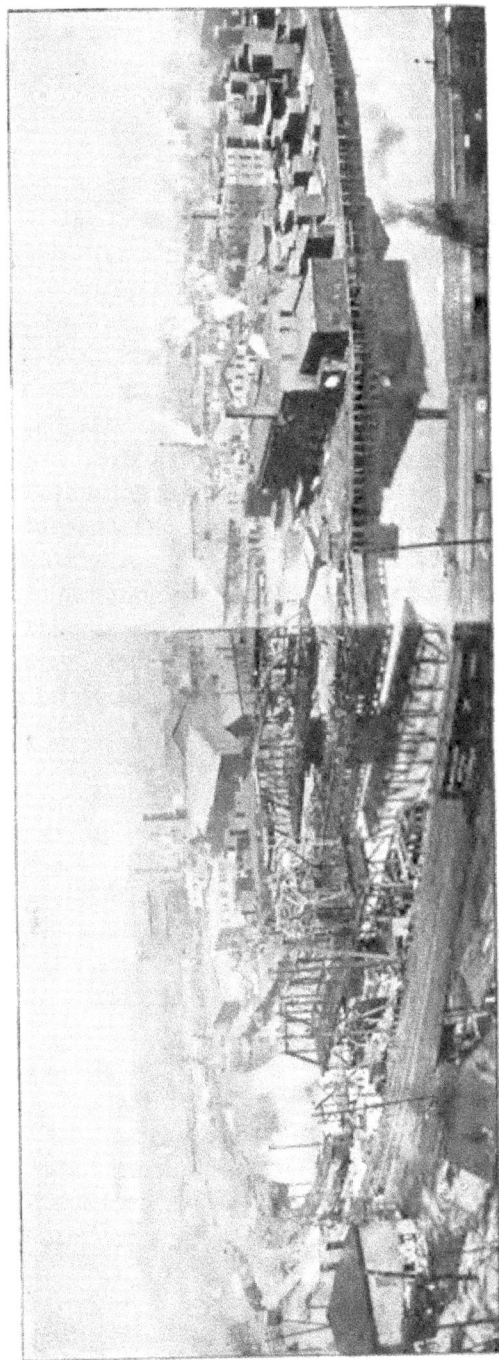

THE CUYAHOGA VALLEY, CLEVELAND, IN 1895.

(Showing double-swing bridge—only one in America.)

THE CITY OF CLEVELAND.

BY F. E. DENTON.

Cleveland, capital of the far-famed Western Reserve, and metropolis of Ohio, is one of the fairest cities of any land. While there are towns which surpass it in certain ways, there are none which combine so many of the features requisite to the conception of an ideal city. Its development has not been paroxysmal or factitious, but healthful and many-sided. It has been indebted to no boom for advancement in any field. Its growth has been the sure unfolding of natural advantages, and it has passed to the proud position of one of the leading commercial centers of the republic. Though engrossed in material activities, its people have never forgotten that trade is only one facet of municipal greatness, and have sacrificed to their wonderful success no advantage of their truer well-being. It is generally understood that urban life is largely artificial, and that a bucolic environment is of best service to man physically, mentally, and morally. Admitting this to be true, it can be said of Cleveland that, above all other great cities, it is the most rural. It unites in singular measure the spirit and stir of city life and the beauty and peace of country life. It unites what is most desirable in both lives, crowning the union with the charm of its own individuality.

Two years are yet to pass before it will be a full century since the sturdy Connecticut surveyor landed upon the banks of the Cuyahoga River, and what was to be Cleveland began. Much sagacity was exhibited by him in his choice of a site for the city which was to bear his name. Cleveland stands upon an undulating plateau, one hundred feet above the waters of Lake Erie. This plateau is cleft north and south by the valley of the Cuyahoga River. This sinuous stream is navigable by the largest vessels a long distance to the southward. The city has a frontage of about sixteen miles upon the river. More than five of these miles are built up in docks. This dockage is utilized in passenger boat landings, warehouses, grain elevators, iron fur-

The Weideman Company,

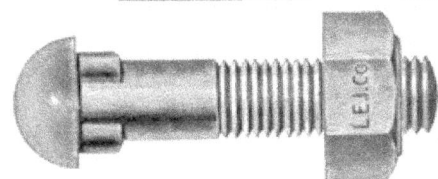

naces, lime kilns, slaughtering and meat-packing establishments, and the handling of vast quantities of iron ore, coal, pig iron, and lumber. Formerly, that portion of the city west of the river—now containing about one-third of its population—was known as Ohio City, being a separate corporation. In 1855, it was united with Cleveland, since which time the union has been rendered perpetual by the stone and iron wedlock of two massive viaducts, each being nearly a mile in length, and both costing nearly $3,500,000. Besides these great bridges, there are numerous smaller ones, so that the two portions of the city enjoy as complete facilities for communication as though they were one in topography, as in interests and destiny. It was not many years ago that the river was the only harbor. In 1825, there were only three feet of water in a narrow and crooked channel at its mouth. To-day, as the result of the improvements made from time to time, and the great breakwaters built by the government, the harbor of Cleveland is one of the finest upon the lakes. The western breakwater is about a mile and a half in length, and it is expected that when the eastern breakwater shall be completed, it will be fully two miles in length. These gigantic arms will encircle an immense basin, wherein the ever-increasing marine business of future generations will be transacted.

Cleveland is a spacious city. Its area is about thirty square miles, including the recently annexed villages of Brooklyn and West Cleveland. It has a frontage of some seven miles upon the lake. The distance between the extreme points within its limits is about ten miles east and west, and seven miles north and south. It may be seen from these figures that its citizens do not need to elbow one another. Though it has increased in population more rapidly than any other Western city in the country, with the exception of Chicago, there are very few of its more than twenty-three hundred streets which can be said to be overcrowded. According to the Eleventh Federal Census, only seventeen per cent. of its population lived over ten in a house, while in New York the percentage reached eighty-three and one-third. It is this roomy character of the city which is one of its most delightful features. It has a direct and important bearing upon municipal peace, beauty, and healthfulness. To this feature is the city indebted for its far-famed width of streets and unequalled opportunities for drainage and sewerage. The water supply, of a

39

remarkably pure character, is drawn from the depths of the lake. This body exerts a gracious influence upon local climatic conditions. In a region noted for extremes of temperature, it plays the part of a meteorological balance-wheel, abating the rigor of Winter and tempering the heat of Summer. It is also claimed for it that it acts as a protection against wind-storms of a destructive character. The climate of Cleveland is less changeable than that of any other city of the same latitude. Nature seems to have the physical well-being of its citizens under especial guardianship, as there are few country places even where the chances of life are better. Last year, the percentage of deaths to each one thousand of population was only 17.43.

Cleveland has had a phenomenal growth, increase having begotten increase, as in the case of the proverbial snow-ball. When the first quarter of a century had sped, it was still only a modest hamlet of 150 souls. It was not until 1830 that it had passed the thousand mark. From that time its growth began in earnest. According to the Federal Census, the population in 1840 was 6,071; in 1850, 17,034; in 1860, 43,830; in 1870, 92,829; in 1880, 160,146, and in 1890, 261,560. At the present time, the population probably exceeds 340,000. At this rate of increase, Cleveland will enter the twentieth century with 430,000 citizens. In 1850, it was the twenty-fifth city in the United States; in 1860, the twentieth; in 1870, the fifteenth; in 1880, the eleventh, and in 1890, the tenth. Within that period, it outstripped the following cities: Lowell, New Haven, Worcester, Syracuse, Providence, Rochester, Louisville, Newark, Milwaukee, Buffalo, Pittsburgh, Richmond, Albany, Detroit, Washington, and New Orleans. Contemplating the miracle of its past, the most ardent dream falls within the circle of probability.

A great city is supposed to be purely a practical institution. It is expected that the smoke and thunder of traffic will displace the æsthetic by a sort of natural right. But in Cleveland the beautiful has ever demanded and received its full share of devotion. Consequently, there is, perhaps, no city of its size in the country so singularly attractive. The proximity of the lake, with its ever-changing aspects, and delicious breezes tempering the hottest of rays; the broad avenues, so embowered with foliage as to have given Cleveland the name of the Forest City; the countless lovely homes, with their green lawns; the picturesque

Y. M. C. A. BUILDING,
Corner Erie and Prospect Streets.

Annual Capacity, ... 250,000 Barrels.

43

resorts, and the rare points of interest, render it a most charming place to visit in the Summer months. It is its manifold attractions and facilities of access by land and sea which have made Cleveland a favorite convention city. Despite the railroad strike and "hard times," it was the meeting place, in 1894, of the greatest of the Christian Endeavor conventions. To meet the ever-increasing demands upon hospitality, the city's hotel capacity has been more than doubled during the last few years, and to-day it boasts of a number of hostelries which are the peers of any. The leading ones are the Hollenden, the Stillman, the Weddell, the Forest City, the Kennard, the American, and the Hawley; but there are many others of considerable capacity. To meet the demand for a large convention hall, Music Hall, which comfortably seats 5,000 people, was built a number of years ago; but its facilities are no longer adequate. The needs in this direction, however, will soon be met, upon the completion of the immense armory of the Ohio National Guard, under process of construction at the corner of Bond and Hamilton Streets. This armory will include an auditorium capable of seating 10,000 people, and then Cleveland will be able to entertain as large a convention as has yet assembled in the land.

THE CITY PARKS.

The park system of the city is one of its chief glories. Monumental Park, containing ten acres, in the heart of the business section, is the oldest of the parks, dating back well toward the beginning of the century. It is adorned with the bronze effigy of General Moses Cleaveland, and with the Soldiers' and Sailors' Monument, one of the grandest and most unique of memorials, built by the county at vast expense, and dedicated with imposing ceremonies on July 4, 1894. Lakeview Park, with its fountains and green banks and rustic bridges, stretches along the slope of the lake bluffs from the foot of Seneca Street to the foot of Erie Street, and is only a short walk from Monumental Park. Half a mile farther east, also near the lake, is Clinton Park. Still farther east, some four miles, is Gordon Park, the bequest of the late W. J. Gordon. This park contains about two hundred acres of meadow, stream, and wood. Nature and art have combined to make of it a marvel of picturesque beauty, and a more charming and restful place could scarcely be imagined.

44

THE LAMSON & SESSIONS CO.

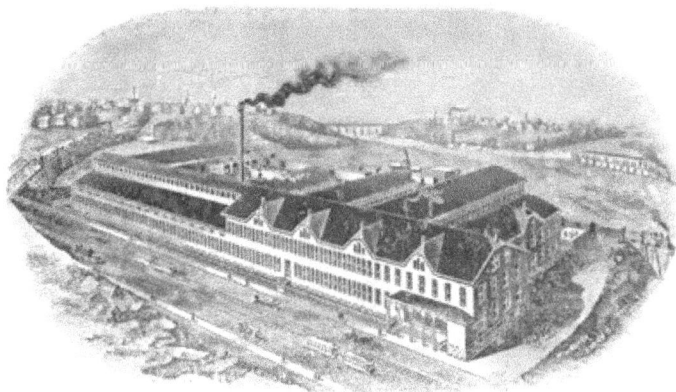

MANUFACTURERS OF

BOLTS, NUTS, RIVETS AND WRENCHES,

CLEVELAND, OHIO.

45

Two miles to the southward is Wade Park, containing seventy acres of glen and hill and grove and field; an artificial lake large enough for boating purposes; a zoological garden; pleasant walks and driveways, and every requisite to a popular resort. It is thronged daily in Spring, Summer, and Autumn. Wade and Gordon Parks are to be wedded in the near future by a splendid boulevard. On the West Side is the new Edgewater Park and Pelton Park, and in the southern suburbs, Forest City Park, all interesting resorts. There are also many lesser places, public and private, scattered through the city, conducive to the pleasant drawing of a long breath. Eighty-one acres have been purchased by the Park Commissioners, in Brooklyn Township, for a park. An extensive and beautiful South End park is contemplated, and will, doubtless, ere long be a reality. The extension of Erie Street into the lake, and the construction of a large tract of land thereon for a pleasure resort, is another project receiving municipal attention. It has also been proposed that the boulevard to be built from Wade Park to Gordon Park be continued from park to park, circumvallating the city with a landscape garden, as it were, and impartially distributing its delights to the people of every section. Euclid Avenue, extending eastward from Monumental Park many miles, aligned with palatial homes, and famous the world over as one of the most magnificent of streets, is in reality a park "long drawn out," having, throughout its attenuation, all of the charms of a sylvan retreat. About a mile east of Wade Park is Lake View Cemetery, where rises skyward the beautiful monument erected to the memory of the martyred President, James A. Garfield, whose mortal remains repose within its crypt.

THE EDUCATIONAL SYSTEM.

The cause of education has ever been dear to the people of Cleveland, and they have done more for it, proportionately, than the people of any other American city. Over sixty massive brick school buildings, equipped with every modern convenience, testify to their deep interest in the intellectual welfare of the rising generations. Within these buildings, an army of more than 40,000 youth are instructed by 850 teachers, skilled in the most enlightened methods. The city pays out a million of dollars annually, and deems the money well spent, for the nurture of the

In placing your orders for printing, patronize an office using this label:

47

minds of its young Aside from the public schools are the parochial schools, Catholic and Lutheran, wherein more than 15,000 children are taught, and the private schools and colleges, which have an attendance of some 5,000 pupils. The leading institution of higher education is Western Reserve University, including Adelbert College, the College for Women, the Cleveland Medical College, the Cleveland School of Law, the College of Dentistry, the Conservatory of Music, and the School of Art. This university is fast coming to be recognized as one of the great centers of learning. The Case School of Applied Science stands in the front rank of scientific schools. The Homœopathic Medical College is one of the oldest and most successful institutions of its kind in the country. The Medical Department of the University of Wooster is also located here. The city's educational facilities are supplemented by two great libraries—the Cleveland Public Library, with 80,000 volumes, and Case Library, with 35,000 volumes. There are over 200 churches and 225 benevolent organizations in the city.

The educational life of Cleveland finds further expression in over one hundred newspapers, magazines, and other periodicals. Among its dailies are the Cleveland *Leader*, the leading Republican journal of the State, with its evening edition, *The News and Herald ;* the *Plain Dealer*, the leading Democratic journal of the State, with its evening edition ; the *Press*, an independent afternoon paper; and the *World*, a Republican afternoon paper, of which Hon. Robert P. Porter, of New York, recently became proprietor. Two dailies—the *Wœchter-Anzeiger* and the *Neüe Presse* —represent the German element of the population. Among literary, society, and trade publications are *The Voice*, an illustrated Sunday paper, *The Clevelander*, *Town Topics*, and *The Iron Trade Review*. There are nearly one hundred printing establishments in the city, whose trade extends to almost every State and Territory in the Union.

NATURAL AND DEVELOPED ADVANTAGES.

The greatness of Cleveland commercially is chiefly due to the marvelous advantages of its situation. It might almost seem as if its matter-of-fact founder were the subject of inspiration in 1796, since there was no way in which he could have apprehended how the future would so signally justify his choice. Certainly,

PERRY'S MONUMENT, WADE PARK.

VIEW IN LAKE VIEW PARK.

Entire New Management

. . . THE . . .

Cleveland World

Robert P. Porter

Having purchased a controlling interest in the above Newspaper, it is proposed to improve and make the World one of the best Republican Newspapers in the United States. . . . .

Under Its New Management

The World will be a Clean, Vigorous, Unique, Up-to-Date Republican Newspaper. . . . .

WHY NOT TRY IT ? . . . .

THE PEOPLE ARE TALKING ABOUT IT.

Politically, the World favors

Protection to American industry and decent wages for American labor. A sound settlement of the financial question on a gold and silver basis. Liberal treatment for the veterans of the war. An aggressive foreign policy. The building up of our merchant marine. . .

It will be a Newspaper for the Home, and expects to Win on its Merits as such.

NEW PRESSES,

NEW TYPESETTING MACHINES,

NEW BUILDING.———

All the News of the World for . . . . **ONE CENT.**

A Cheap, Bright, Gossipy, Newsy Paper for the Masses.

———Address, THE WORLD, CLEVELAND.

the earth-hidden riches of the Southwest and Northwest could not have entered into his calculations. Yet, so far as results are concerned, it is as if his eye could have seen the future with the clearness of a present reality. The traffic of the inland seas with a large section, comprising the most populous and opulent part of the Union, gravitates to Cleveland. It is the naturally-appointed meeting place of fleets and railroads. From the mines of Michigan, Minnesota, and Wisconsin, comes more than one-half of the raw product for the iron and steel industries of the entire country, a large part of which is brought to Cleveland. From the forest regions of the same States comes the material for countless habitations. From the bituminous coal fields of Ohio and Pennsylvania come millions of tons of the very best fuel. Eleven railroads, operating 5,237 miles of track—considerably more railway mileage than there is in the kingdom of Sweden—meet the laden navies at Cleveland, where they exchange their riches. The fact that it is such a great distributing point for the mineral nourishment of civilization has been a wonderful stimulus to manufactures, and, as the result, Cleveland enjoys a diversification of industry almost unparalleled. There are few useful things which the wit of man has devised which it does not make. It has more than three thousand manufacturing establishments, great and small. Many of these employ a small army of men. More than half of the population are directly engaged in productive labor.

Cleveland enjoys the prestige of being the largest shipbuilding port in the United States. In fact, there is only one district in the world—the famous Clyde district, in Great Britain—in which the new tonnage turned out each year is in excess of that built here. Cleveland's steel ships are among the finest merchant vessels on the globe. This city also enjoys the honor of owning more floating property than any other city on the continent, with the exception of New York. Its vessels will aggregate in value $18,000,000. The cities of the world whose maritime commerce exceeds that of Cleveland could be counted on the fingers of a hand. The value of its lake trade in 1894 was $55,000,000. Its commerce, especially in coal and iron ore, practically includes the business of several other ports east and west. It matters little at what port of Lake Erie the cargo may be discharged, the contract of sale, the delivery, and the payment are Cleveland transactions.

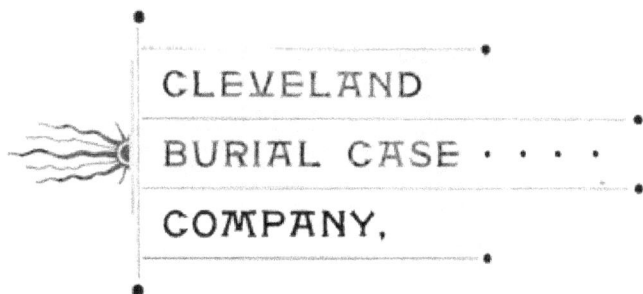

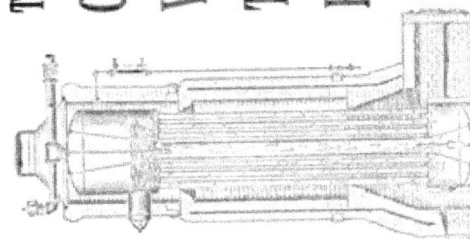

In the manufacture of heavy forgings, wire nails, nuts and bolts, carriage and wagon hardware, vapor stoves, sewing machines, steel-tired car wheels, and heavy street railway machinery, Cleveland is foremost of American cities. It is the headquarters of the malleable iron industry. In this city, the greatest shoddy mills of America are located; also an electric light carbon works, having an annual capacity of ten million carbons. Cleveland leads the world in the manufacture of petroleum products. It makes the largest telescopes. It ranks next to New York and Chicago as a market for millinery. It makes more than half of the gum chewed by the human race. Not only do its multiform industries furnish employment to an ever-increasing host of toilers, but it pays them good wages, as compared with other cities. As a dwelling place for the man who earns his bread by the sweat of his brow, its advantages are many and marked.

The financial system of Cleveland comprises some fifty banking institutions, including national banks, savings banks, state banking companies, and saving and loan associations. About half of these institutions are savings banks, a single one of which has resources aggregating to exceed $24,000,000. The deposits of Cleveland banks will aggregate to exceed $65,000,000. The record of the city's financial system has been a most creditable one. No speculative influences have gone to swell the volume of its business. A rare freedom from failures or serious disturbances has characterized it. The direct outgrowth of the city's wonderful commercial interests, in the attitude of a grateful child to its parent, it has ever encouraged their onward and upward progress by its liberal policy. The great bulk of its savings deposits has been invested in building homes for mechanics and others of moderate means. Consequently, there is no great city where so many of the inhabitants own their own homes. In that part of the year when building is most active, every setting sun witnesses the addition to the city of enough comfortable residences to make a handsome hamlet. Streets are springing up as if by magic, and the city is creeping into the country on every side. There are very few places where residence property can be purchased at a cheaper figure. The most desirable manufacturing property can be secured at prices from thirty-five to fifty per cent. cheaper than in other cities of its class. Cleveland has been free from

To the Republican League Clubs
THE LEADER Extends Greeting and
A Welcome Most Cordial.
An Unrivaled News-gathering Service
Both Telegraphic and Local,
And Bright, Honest, Fearless
Editorial Comment on the
Live Questions of the Day make

THE MORNING LEADER,

THE SUNDAY LEADER,

THE NEWS AND HERALD

Eagerly Sought for as the
Foremost Republican Newspapers
Of Ohio, and the
Advertising Mediums par Excellence.
As a Gatherer of Legitimate News
THE CLEVELAND LEADER Stands
Easily First and Foremost in its Field.
The Leader is Rightly Named.

real estate booms, as of all other kinds. The market for land has been active, but healthfully so. A great stimulus to the growth of the city has been its comprehensive and unrivalled street car system, comprising 200 miles of track. Horse cars have become a memory, and electric and cable cars so neutralize time as to bring the remotest citizen within a half hour of the City Hall. The Cleveland Chamber of Commerce, one of the strongest and most vigorous commercial organizations in the country, is an active factor in developing and energizing every effort and movement promotive of the best interests of the city.

A UNIQUE MUNICIPAL SYSTEM.

Any description of Cleveland would be incomplete which did not mention its admirable system of government. This has attracted a great deal of attention throughout the country, since it was, in an emphatic sense, a "new departure." There is more or less danger attending political experiments, and the average citizen is not disposed to look upon them with favor; but "the Federal plan," as it is called, has, during the four years of its operation, thoroughly established itself in popular approval, and illustrated the wisdom of its originators. It receives its name from the fact that it is closely patterned after the plan of the Federal Government. Its distinctive feature is that it centers authority and fixes responsibility. Under "the Federal plan," the executive power is in the hands of a Mayor (elected by the people) and his cabinet, consisting of six heads of departments, chosen by him and confirmed by the Council. Following are the heads of the departments: The Director of Law, who is corporation counsel; the Director of Public Works, who has charge of the water works, streets, parks, public buildings, and all improvements thereon and additions thereto; the Directors of Police and Fire Service, whose duties are fully indicated by their titles; the Director of Accounts, who is city auditor, and has full control of the book-keeping and reports of all the departments; and the Director of Charities and Correction, who is responsible for the care of the work-house, infirmary, and cemeteries. The Mayor and Directors constitute the Board of Control, whose duties and powers correspond in a general way with those of the boards of improvement in other cities. The head of each department has full authority to select all of its officers and employes, and to

57

purchase its supplies. His appointments do not require confirmation. The Mayor can remove any member of his cabinet at pleasure, who, in turn, has the power to remove any subordinate of his department. All legislative authority is in the hands of a Council of twenty members, who are elected from districts. The appropriations are made as in Congress. No warrant can be drawn on an exhausted fund, and the revenues cannot be anticipated or used for any other purpose or period than is provided by the appropriation act. The judicial officers—the Police Judge and Police Prosecutor—are elected by popular vote. "The Federal plan" went into operation in the Spring of 1891. In the Spring of 1892, a reorganization act for the government of the public schools of the city was passed by the State Legislature. By its provisions, a Director of Schools and a School Council of seven members are elected by the people. The Director has all executive control, and all appointments are made by him, except those of teachers, who are appointed by the Superintendent of Instruction. The School Council has control of all legislation for the schools. The City Auditor is the auditor of the School Department. The new government has most admirably fulfilled all that its most earnest advocates could have hoped for it. It has been safe and economical, and its operations open as the day. It is not too much to say that it has materially contributed to the progress of the city.

The honor of Mayor—a very high one considering the great responsibility attaching to that position under the new regime —has been bestowed upon three citizens, namely: Hon. William G. Rose, Republican, elected in 1891; Hon. Robert Blee, Democrat, elected in 1893; and Hon. Robert E. McKisson, Republican, elected in 1895. The latter is said to be the youngest man ever entrusted with the executive authority of a great city, being only thirty-two years of age.

RAILWAY LINES.

The following railway lines have passenger depots at Cleveland: Lake Shore & Michigan Southern; depot, foot of Water Street. Cleveland & Pittsburg; depot, foot of Water Street. Cleveland, Canton & Southern; depot, No. 341 Ontario Street. Big Four; depot, foot of Water Street. Cleveland, Lorain & Wheeling; depot, foot of Water Street. Mt. Vernon & Pan

BALL'S STANDARD BUSINESS MAN'S WATCH.

We take pleasure in submitting for your attention our new small size thin model "Ball's Standard Watch" as above illustrated. We have spent much time and money in developing and perfecting this watch to its present standard of excellence, and can recommend them highly to anyone seeking a time-piece. Perfect time-keepers are now the requirement of the day and a business man whose time is valuable cannot afford to be without a reliable watch. They are up to date in every detail. **GARFIELD SOUVENIR SPOONS.**

THE WEBB C. BALL CO.,
Watch and Diamond Merchants,

Ball Building. Cor. Superior and Seneca Sts.,   CLEVELAND, OHIO.

ASK FOR IT!   ORDER IT!

America's Best Beer,

THE **BARTHOLOMAY**

ROCHESTER!

ON DRAUGHT AND IN BOTTLES.

Cleveland Branch :

76 MICHIGAN ST.   Telephone 2000.

Handle Route; depot, foot of Water Street. Nickel Plate; depot Broadway, east of Cross Street. New York, Lake Erie & Western; depot, foot of South Water Street. Valley; depot, foot of South Water Street. The Cleveland headquarters of the Baltimore & Ohio are at No. 143 Superior Street; of the Cleveland Belt & Terminal, at No. 341 Ontario Street; of the Cleveland & Mahoning Valley, 38 Mercantile Bank building; of the New York, Pennsylvania & Ohio, No. 30 Euclid Avenue; and of the Pennsylvania, No. 155 St Clair Street.

PASSENGER STEAMER LINES.

One of the most attractive features of the Summer life in Cleveland is the opportunities afforded for excursions by water of any desired length. Handsome and capacious steamers make frequent trips to suburban resorts on the lake shore; daily trips are made by splendid steamers of the largest size to Put-in-Bay, Kelley's Island, and Lakeside. Daily trips are also made to Buffalo and Detroit, making close connections with through railway trains; and if the seeker for pleasure or health desires a longer voyage, he can take a thousand mile run on magnificently appointed water craft to Duluth or Chicago, with stop-off privileges at Mackinac or the Sault. The passenger traffic of the Great Lakes is rapidly increasing as the beauties and advantages of these inland ocean trips become better known, and the various steamship lines are sparing no expense to accommodate this traffic and to make this form of pleasuring attractive.

The following passenger boat lines have landings at Cleveland: Detroit & Cleveland Steam Navigation Co.; foot of Superior Street. Cleveland & Buffalo Transit Company; foot of St. Clair Street. Anchor Line; No. 107 to No. 115 River Street. Northern Steamship Line; No. 23 River Street.

Points of interest in and about the city may be reached by the street car lines of the Cleveland Electric Railway Company and the Cleveland City Railway Company, from Monumental Park, in the heart of the business section, as follows: Garfield Memorial, Lake View Cemetery, and Wade Park, Euclid Avenue car; Gordon Park, St. Clair Street car; Rocky River and Edgewater Park, Detroit Street car; the new park in Brooklyn township, Pearl Street car; Forest City Park, Broadway car; Berea, Lorain Street car.

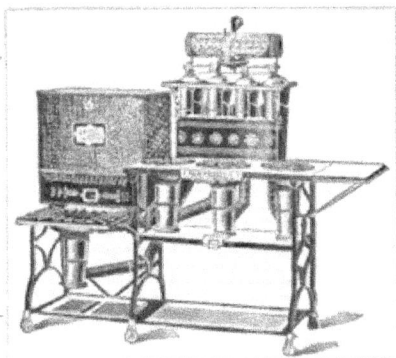

A VIEW IN EUCLID AVENUE.

PIERS AND ENTRANCE TO CLEVELAND HARBOR.

www.ingramcontent.com/pod-product-compliance
Lightning Source LLC
Chambersburg PA
CBHW021629270326
41931CB00008B/942